A Good
Hard to Find

(part 2 of *Selfies*)

a poem in six parts

Ronnie Ferguson

Harvard Square Press
Cambridge, Massachusetts

Harvard Square Press
Cambridge, MA
United States of America
ISBN: 9798325857546
Cover Photo by Daniel Ferguson
Cover Design by Ronnie Ferguson

Harvard Square Press
Cambridge, Massachusetts

harvardsquarepress.com

A Good Fight is Hard to Find

(part 2 of *Selfies*)

CONTENTS

A Good Fight is Hard to Find

I. <u>Liars in the Library</u>

i'd learned a secret or two
about how to get the mob
on my side

i mocked you in class
told everyone you wore girly nails
probably painted them at home
prancing around
in your momma's dresses

to this day i couldn't say
how or why
i first got hung up on you
besides your name
and the press-on nails commercials
but that doesn't fully explain
why i picked you

we were hillbilly kids
with hillbilly houses
and hand-me-down clothes

we could've been cousins

you could've called me
Ronald McDonald
or something akin
to a wet willy
and moved on

but you stayed quiet
sometimes ignoring me
and the others laughing
sometimes blushing

even when i knew i got you good
i didn't stop

one Monday morning
you'd had enough and turned
a cold eye to me
suggested we settle things
after lunch on the playground

i laughed at the challenge
wondered if you knew
who the hell you were talking to
i was undefeated
in playground fights
and certain i'd make quick work of you
before the playground ladies
knew what was happening
inside the three-to-five-rows-deep
circle of our classmates
who'd been trying
with gobs of gossip
to get our bout on the cards
since winter

you sat alone at lunch

i sat with the mob
and we all made faces at you
but you didn't make any faces back

on the sidewalk to the playground
i confided in my two toughest
most trusted friends

> *guys i don't know about this*
> *he might have brass knuckles*
> *or try to kick me in the nuts*
> *if he does something*
> *you better have my back*
> *if he gets me in a lucky hold*
> *pull him off*

even though talking heads had me
beating you nine out of ten times
i was unnerved by unknowns (something
i'd never had time to consider
since most of my fights broke out
midgame)

as much as i loved the thrill of victory
i hated how the adrenaline rush
hit before a fight

> heart thumping
> shaky bones
> tingling all over

my boys promised
to step in
if i needed help
so i strutted
flanked by my bodyguards
as the mob led the way
to a patch of torn-up grass
near the monkey bars

the mob parted

you met me in the center
      and said *let's go*

i tried to lock your head
and arm
but you pushed me off
landed your first punch
to my temple

as i fell to one knee
you stepped in closer
and threw a right uppercut
barely missing my jaw

the ring you wore
cut my ear at the bottom

i got to my feet
      dizzy
            bleeding

you grabbed my shirt
as i signaled for my bodyguards
to sneak attack you from behind
but they just kept shouting for more
with the others
while you put your nose to my nose
and asked with a smile
      had enough yet

      your mama hasn't had enough i said

you swung again
glancing the other side of my head

before the playground ladies
finally swooped in

i'd never been punched before
in fact
i didn't even know how
to throw a punch
i'd steered all my previous fights
to wrestling matches
which was more my style

i didn't cry

but i wanted to

30 minutes later
our class in the library
i was still trying to process
where i went wrong
and why i couldn't close the distance

then your name came over the intercom
and you were off to the principal's office

i searched for a book
as my thoughts drifted
back to my home
        my bedroom
                the quiet place
                        under my blanket

i was shaking
knowing i was next
so i snuck away from the class
to sit at a table in the corner

pretend to read
about giant squids

my two bodyguards found me
pat my back
talking all fast
man you kicked his ass (that was great) he deserved it

  whaaaaat i replied

you really kicked his ass
he only got you good
with that faggy skull ring
but you had a hold on him
(has your ear stopped bleeding)

  yeah i said

you're still the champ
they insisted

  what do you mean
  i lost guys
  i lost

we were there
(you won)

  i lost guys
  i got my ass kicked

whatever man
that's not what we've been telling everyone
to say

i gotta piss i lied
and turned toward the bathroom
just as i was summoned
by my birth name
over the intercom

Lee
i'm sure you already know
i swatted away
every false rumor
took the L
clean on the chin
cuz you got me good
and i had it coming
and i think it was for the best
i didn't run with those guys
ever again

II. Black Sabbath Birthday Blues

you told the principal
the playground ladies got it wrong
it was just a friendly match
between friends
so i never got to admit my big mouth
was the problem
as i was planning

      within a week
      all our fans
      had forgotten us
      and our fight

the next month
my birthday came around
and it was just the two of us
standing on the sidewalk
after school on a Friday
when my dad rolled up
in his El Camino

      earlier in the week i'd overheard
      pieces of my mom's conversation
      with my dad on the phone
      but nothing was conclusive

      we put the pieces together
      at recess
      and decided
      somehow my dad knew somebody
      who knew somebody
      in the underground
      with free tickets

for a special concert
reuniting Black Sabbath with Ozzy

on the drive out of town
the three of us took turns
picking songs on the radio
while we shared
the leftover cupcakes
from class

my dad asked about your family
if you had any brothers or sisters
if you went to church
or played any sports

though you were my new best friend
i must admit
i didn't know much about you
we'd found ourselves
lonely
in a relationship of necessity
before i'd fully healed from our fight

the parking lot at the sports arena
was only a quarter full
there wasn't a barrel fire
a keg
or a mohawk in sight

the preshow party
must've moved around back
i thought but didn't say
cuz i knew my dad
recently gave up drinking

though i sometimes talked
tough at school
as if i were a heavyweight
i'd never had
more than a sip
from a can of warm beer
somebody left
on a table somewhere

now boys
i want you on your best behavior
i don't mind if you have a little fun
but don't go gettin' too wild

is Black Sabbath here already (is
Ozzy gonna bite a bat)
we blurted
tripping over each other

even better he said
handing us each a ticket
and a $10 bill
before motioning us
to run ahead

we raced to the doors
nearly pissing our pants

rock music blared from below
but it wasn't a live band yet

the bottom floor
was only beginning to fill out
along with a few clusters
in higher sections

we figured we still had time
to scour the crowd
for pretty girls and famous people
so we high-stepped it
to concessions
like a couple goofy brothers
who never got out of the house

my dad found us
and led the way to our seats
far to the left
in the front row of the upper deck

we might've insisted moving
closer considering
all the empty seats below
but he explained
boys
i chose this spot
so we could take it all in

    look around

    he was right
    the whole place was ours

    it made us feel like little gods
    in some grand balcony

the lights went out
around the arena
and a spotlight came up
on a clean-shaven man
in a turquoise suit

he stepped center stage
and at the same time
appeared in a close-up
on the giant screen
above his head

the crowd roared
clearly they knew him
but we didn't have any idea
who he was

we threw our fists in the air
and yelled anyway

i take it y'all saw my last fight
he said with an easy smile
and a knowing nod
bet y'all know that dude
was ranked #3 in the world
before i knocked him out
sent him back
to the undercard

but what some of y'all don't know is
i grew up a couple blocks from here
my daddy's
still pastor of the church
'cross the street
same church
i's baptized in

there was a time
after i lost a few
i almost   almost

almost hung up my gloves
and joined daddy
in ministry
but the Lord had another plan
thanks be to Him

thanks be to you
i'm next in line for a title shot

nothing'd make me happier
than to bring home the belt
to share with y'all

ain't no place like home
he proclaimed
wagging his finger
ain't no place like home

the crowd went nuts again

we glanced at each other

our cheers were half-hearted

now the Lord may use me
as a preacher someday
when time's right for Him
but i'm not here
to talk about me
and my accomplishments
nope
i'm here to introduce a guy
who's an even bigger hit
with Jesus

he even played Jesus
on Broadway
in Jesus Christ Superstar
he's been on the cover of TIME
that's right TIME

and it's time now
ladies and gentlemen
boys and girls
please help me welcome a man
who's a world-famous singer
former member of Black Sabbath
a Spirit-filled evangelist
and a deep brother
from another-color mother

the one

the only

we didn't recognize the name

it wasn't Ozzy

the arena erupted
as the boxer walked offstage
and the singing evangelist
took his place

i squirmed in my seat
and thought there was a good chance
you'd never forgive me
and dump me as a friend

this would go down
like a stinky deuce
the worst
birthday ever

my dad leaned forward
as the singing evangelist
shared the story of his former life
on the dark side
and how he came to faith

i passed you Peanut M&M's
without saying a word

my appetite had left the building

by the time he finished
we were so bored
i wondered if maybe
Heaven was a place
where fun means no fun
kids get in free
but there's no kids menu
birthday candles
are actually firecrackers
        double-chocolate cake
        all over the golden walls
        for eternity

his band crashed in
after altar call
and most the crowd
stood and clapped
swaying to the music

my dad said we could walk around
if we wanted
but to meet him back at our seats
before the end

aglow in our freedom
we stole a stack of extra programs
and ended up
in about the same seats
on the opposite side of the arena

as worship grew more intense
we made a squadron
of paper airplanes

one by one
we sent them raining like manna
on the worshipers below

and my special day was saved
from the boring plans of Hell

III. The Myth of the Lone Apple-Chucker

that summer you invited me
to spend the night
for your 11th birthday

we camped out in your attic
with a new porno mag

you laughed when you flipped
to the first butthole
and explained
it can be easy to mistake
in the heat of the moment
being so close
to the honeypot

> this was as new to me
> as the first day
> at a new school

though you'd won our fight
you never felt the need to rub it in
you had a wise older-brother air
i admired
the only problem was
when you got going on something
i couldn't tell if you were serious
or just messing

the demon
answering our questions
on the Ouija board
was named Zom
though i had my suspicions

you never cracked a smile
or admitted moving
the planchette

we were on your turf

at my house our roles reversed

while my dad slept
on the couch
i challenged you
to a game of Penis Chicken
        whoever could stand for longest
        with penis in hand
        directly in front of my snoring dad
        would win

and the next afternoon
when he left to run errands
we chucked apples at passing cars
then hid in the bathroom
when a cop snooped around the house
and yelled for us
a few steps inside the front door

for a long time after
we spun a tall tale
saying my dad had showed up
as we were being cuffed
and he punched out
the cop in the driveway
setting us free
(back at school
we even acted out the scene
for a few kids in the cafeteria)

but after the cop left
without finding us
he paid a visit to my mom
at work

she showed up livid
and spanked me
right in front of you

i told her
i'd acted alone

the couple
with the baby in the front seat
declined to press charges
when my mom offered to replace
their cracked windshield

she dropped you at your house
without tattling to your parents

IV. <u>Rope-a-Dope</u>

i don't know if you recall that night
we stood in front of my dad
penises in hand
it's been a regret that returns
to me in nightmares
i wake up bound in the shame of Ham
desperately wishing i'd been a decent son
like Shem or Japheth

you never really knew
my dad
or the great longing i had
to be close to him
it seemed he was always fighting
bad habits
or working on projects
to help some less fortunate family
or the church

he made sure i had video games
treats (mostly Fruit by the Foot)
Hammer pants
a leather jacket
but i don't think he ever understood
i would've traded
all the gifts in the world
for a weekly father/son cliché
tossing the pigskin in the park
barbecuing in the backyard

    or whatever

      anything

in winter i couldn't wait
for the New Year New Life
weekend church retreat
cuz my dad told me
there'd be plenty of time
for fun

he encouraged me
to invite you
to try out the new sled
i got for Christmas
do you remember that thing

                    three skis and a steering wheel

he told us to be careful
it was so fast
a kid in Colorado died
when his hit a tree

we found out the first night
we were the only two
young people
besides a toddler
whose mom worked in hospitality
for the retreat center

after meals adults broke
for small group activities
while we were sent away
to explore

we tried to break in
to the locked gym

and got yelled at
by a crusty janitor

when Sunday came
i was wishing
i'd read the weekend schedule
before agreeing to attend
there were no group events
that kept us with adults
besides an ice cream outing

    so we spent most of our time sledding

by early afternoon
we were old pros
on the steepest side

teasing between us
turned aggressive.
which led to red-faced wrestling
in the snow

we wondered if anyone
would ever join us outside

as we packed snow ramps
a cold silence set in

we took turns
making modifications
as our jumps grew
dangerously high

      but we still landed
      each one with ease

you packed more snow
on the biggest ramp

by the time i got to the top of the hill
it was three times higher

> you stepped to the side
> threw your fist in the air

without hesitation
i got a running start
hopped on
and steered my sled
to the sweet spot

at the last second
i glanced your way

> airborne
> i gripped the steering wheel
> as my stomach
>> negotiated
>>> with gravity

>> i would've stuck the landing

> if i hadn't been leaning
to one side

the left ski hit first
> flipping me off
> like a cowboy
>> thrown from his horse

                                        the sled slid to a stop
                                        under a pine tree
                                        about 25 yards away

you okay
you called out

i didn't move
or say anything

you ran to me
in a panic
and got on all fours
like a football coach
worried about
his star running back

hey man
you okay
you asked
shaking me

but i just groaned
so you'd stop
whispered
go   get   my   dad

        you set off to find him

i kept my eyes closed
the whole time

        you must've sprinted
        cuz a few minutes later
        i heard his voice

when i opened my eyes
he was there
to help me to my feet

he brought me indoors
to sit with him
at the men's Bible study

i never left his side
while you wandered around

                         alone
                         the rest of the afternoon

it breaks my heart to tell you this
old friend
but you should know
i was never hurt
by the crash
that afternoon

i just needed you
to go away
so i could be healed

V. <u>Wobble Street</u>

in middle school
we'd see each other
but our friendship got lost
in new hallways
eventually
we each found a circle
to run in
though they never touched

sophomore year of high school
i walked out from algebra class
into a mob
standing around
a frisbee-size pool of blood
on the floor
only seconds after a fight
between you and some senior

they said
when you hit him
he went down hard
and when he tried to stand
he was on wobble street
like when Mike Tyson
put the hurt
on Trevor Berbick

i wondered who
said what
to set the other off
and if
i still had your phone number
written down

somewhere
at home

VI. T.K.O.

but i never would've called
cuz i was in my own fight
with God
over things
too stupid to mention

we graduated high school

15 years passed for me
like a sleepless weekend
of madness and grace

> Y2K failed
> to live up to the hype

> the Pistons won a trophy in 2004

> i got married
> and helped make a baby
> and then a divorce

>> somewhere
>> you were living your life

recently
my son and i stopped for lunch
at a sports bar
in your old neighborhood

the bartender was a classmate
from elementary school

she was probably at our fight
that day on the playground
but i didn't bring it up

      as soon as she recognized me
      she gave me a hug
      and we took turns
      offering details
      from our lives
      as we reflected upon
      how strange it is
      to be adults
      with kids of our own
      (she has five
      God bless her)

after a couple rounds of
      who you still friends with
      who lost their hair
      who got arrested
      who got famous
she asked if i remembered you

i nodded and assumed
from the tenderness
in her voice
she was gonna tell me
the two of you
got married

i was armed and ready
with a choice snippet
from one of our golden adventures
even though i hadn't been invited
to the wedding

but she shook her head
hardly believing

    a few months before
    a cop found you dead
    in your car at the park
    near our old middle school

    she'd heard
    there'd been a divorce
    followed by
    a custody battle

    and you'd shot yourself

i caught sight of my son
waiting for me
by the pool table
but i couldn't stand
couldn't find my voice

i longed to hold your face
in my hands
as a twin might
to his brother
i longed with an ache
to get on all fours
whisper in your ear
i love you old friend
and i'll always love you

i imagined us at that same park
in summer

laughing with our kids
and holding them in our arms

just two dorky dads
teaching them
there are many ways to fight
and so many lovely things
worth fighting for
even when it feels like
a good fight is hard to find
with our futures decided
long before the final bell
cuz we're all on our own
in some messed up
Mayweather vs. McGregor Money Fight
minus the money

for days after i couldn't focus
on my son
or my thankless mindless job
cleaning toilets

shit piled up
from here to everywhere

i couldn't eat more than a slice of bread
somebody left
on a table somewhere

i sat with my only photograph
of the two of us
contemplating how
in this violent unforgiving world
even the legends get a raw deal

for a time
everyone remembers them
standing in the ring
holding up their belt

      but   years   pass

they become old guys
covering up in the corner
in a rising contender's highlight reel

just when i couldn't
take any more punishment
from some blind spot
behind my heart
        the force of an old saying
        hit me all at once
        and cleared my cobwebs

i found its truth
to be greater than any memory
we might dig out for our grandkids
greater than any church's presumption
of damnation
for those who take their own lives

why am i telling you all these stories
from our time together
      i mean
      you were there Lee

you're still here too

once a champ
always a champ

ABOUT THE AUTHOR

Ronnie Ferguson has presented his creative and scholarly work internationally. A former King Chavez Parks Fellow and President of the Graduate Writing Association, his artistic endeavors span the genres of poetry, music, film, theatre, and the visual arts.

STREAKING IN TONGUES, the music project he shares with his son, has released nine critically acclaimed albums. The duo have most recently collaborated with saxophonist Patrick Booth on an instrumental album, *Einstein's Napkin*, as well as a trilogy of Bigfoot-themed music and spoken word albums with the two-time Poet Laureate of Michigan's Upper Peninsula, Marty Achatz.

Through his work in film, Ronnie has garnered multiple awards for directing, screenwriting, and acting. His full-length documentaries—*Reflections of an American Sunrise*, *Bigfoot and Marty*, and *3-Day Novice*—explore the writing life and feature readings and interviews with various notable poets, such as the 23rd United States Poet Laureate, Joy Harjo. Most recently, he directed *Tracks of Freedom*, a feature film and miniseries focused on the life and ministry of B.T. Roberts, the founder of the Free Methodist Church.

Along with fellow Upper Peninsula poets, Ronnie co-founded and continues to co-organize The International 3-Day Poetry Chapbook Contest and The Great Lakes Poetry Festival. He teaches at Northern Michigan University and regularly leads community poetry workshops.

A Good Fight is Hard to Find is his second book, the second in the *Selfies* series.

ALSO FROM HARVARD SQUARE PRESS

Lamprey by Erika Kielsgard
Animal Heart by Sam Moe
A Brief Report On The Human Animal by Kathleen M.
      Heideman
On Natural Things by Beth Roberts
When I Was a Fire by Ronnie Ferguson
Jazzing with Bigfoot by Marty Achatz / STREAKING IN
      TONGUES
Love Potions, Teas, Incantations by Beverly Matherne
Undone with Wonder by Helen Haskell Remien
Our Natural Satellite by Russell Brakefield
Conjuring a Ghost & Others Ways to Ruin Your Teeth
      by Randi Clemens
Already Becoming by Zoa Coudret
Christmas with Bigfoot by Marty Achatz / STREAKING IN
      TONGUES
Slow Dancing with Bigfoot by Marty Achatz / STREAKING IN
      TONGUES
History's a Hoot by Cassie G.
Tiger Island by Reagan M. Sova
This Volcano by Cassie G.
Tsar Bomba by Jonas Fox

Harvard Square Press
Cambridge, Massachusetts

harvardsquarepress.com

62584786R00026